Santa Claus

Bobbie Kalman

Crabtree Publishing Company

www.crabtreebooks.com

Created by Bobbie Kalman

For Dexter Crabtree,
who loves Santa Claus all year long!

Author and Editor-in-Chief
Bobbie Kalman

Reading consultant
Elaine Hurst

Editors
Kathy Middleton
Crystal Sikkens

Design
Bobbie Kalman
Katherine Berti

Photo research
Bobbie Kalman

**Production coordinator
and Prepress technician**
Katherine Berti

Illustrations
Barbara Bedell: pages 3 (helper, toys, reindeer, and sleigh), 6, 7, 8, 9, 14, 15 (bottom right)

Photographs
iStockphoto: page 10 (girl)
Other photographs by Shutterstock

Library and Archives Canada Cataloguing in Publication

Kalman, Bobbie, 1947-
    Santa Claus / Bobbie Kalman.

(My world)
ISBN 978-0-7787-9505-6 (bound).--ISBN 978-0-7787-9530-8 (pbk.)

    1. Santa Claus--Juvenile literature. I. Title. II. Series: My world (St. Catharines, Ont.)

GT4992.K335 2011   j394.2663   C2010-901972-5

Library of Congress Cataloging-in-Publication Data

Kalman, Bobbie.
  Santa Claus / Bobbie Kalman.
        p. cm. -- (My world)
  ISBN 978-0-7787-9530-8 (pbk. : alk. paper) -- ISBN 978-0-7787-9505-6 (reinforced library binding : alk. paper)
  1. Santa Claus--Juvenile literature. I. Title. II. Series.

GT4992.K34 2011
394.2663--dc22

2010011299

Crabtree Publishing Company

www.crabtreebooks.com   1-800-387-7650

Printed in Hong Kong/042011/BK20110304

Copyright © **2011 CRABTREE PUBLISHING COMPANY.** All rights reserved. No part of this publication may be reproduced, stored in a retrieval system or be transmitted in any form or by any means, electronic, mechanical, photocopying, recording, or otherwise, without the prior written permission of Crabtree Publishing Company. In Canada: We acknowledge the financial support of the Government of Canada through the Canada Book Fund for our publishing activities.

Published in Canada
Crabtree Publishing
616 Welland Ave.
St. Catharines, Ontario
L2M 5V6

Published in the United States
Crabtree Publishing
PMB 59051
350 Fifth Avenue, 59th Floor
New York, New York 10118

Published in the United Kingdom
Crabtree Publishing
Maritime House
Basin Road North, Hove
BN41 1WR

Published in Australia
Crabtree Publishing
386 Mt. Alexander Rd.
Ascot Vale (Melbourne)
VIC 3032

Words to know

chimney — Christmas Eve — Earth

 gift

helper

reindeer — sleigh

stocking — toys

Santa Claus is coming soon.
He comes on **Christmas Eve.**

You look for him and cannot wait, but he comes while you sleep.

Santa lives at the cold North Pole. His **helpers** live there, too.

They work hard to make great **toys** for me and you and you.

Santa puts
the children's toys
all into his **sleigh**.
He laughs out loud,
waves goodbye,
and soon is on his way.

Up above **Earth** his **reindeer** fly!
They fly very high in the sky.

Do you wait for Santa Claus?
Did you hang your **stocking** yet?
Did you leave some cookies and milk for him?
Santa gets hungry, I'll bet!

Down the **chimney** Santa slides and leaves some toys for you. He reads your note, drinks the milk, and eats some cookies, too.

When morning comes, you get up and cheer. "Look at the **gifts**! Santa was here."

How does your family spend Christmas each year?

Activity

The pictures below show how people thought Santa looked long ago.

Draw your own
picture of Santa.
Will your Santa look
like one of the Santas
in this book?

Notes for adults

Objectives
- to allow children to share their experiences about Santa
- to explore rhyme and encourage children to write rhyming verses

Prerequisite
A map of the world or globe

Question before reading *Santa Claus*
"What can you tell me about Santa Claus?"

Questions after reading book
"Where does Santa Claus live?"
"Can you find the North Pole on this map (globe)?"
"When does Santa Claus come?"
"Who makes the toys at Santa's workshop?"
"To whom is Santa waving goodbye?"
"How does Santa deliver the toys and other gifts? Does he fly on a plane?"
"What treat does Santa like you to leave for him?"
"Does your family celebrate Christmas?"
"How are your family traditions the same or different from those of your friends?"
"How does your community celebrate Christmas?"

Activity
People around the world imagine Santa in different ways.
Ask the children to draw their own pictures of Santa. Tell them to use their imagination and create new "looks" for Santa. Display the pictures of Santa on a bulletin board.

Extension: Rhyme along
Read the book out loud and ask the children to call out the rhyming word that goes with each verse.
Examples of rhymes: sleigh, way; fly, sky; you, too; yet, bet; cheer, here, year; show, ago; look, book.
Look at the book below, *Santa Claus from A to Z*, with the children. Talk about the pictures in the book with them.

With this fun book and your help, children can create their own ABC book about Santa. Each child could draw one or two pictures for the book, such as cookies, decorations, elves, or gifts.

For teacher's guide, go to www.crabtreebooks.com/teachersguides